The *Stepmom* **Retreat**

31 Day Devotional & Guided Journal, with coloring pages for STEPMOMS

Marcee Woodard

This retreat belongs to:

_____

a very special lady

The Stepmom Retreat

How to Use this Book

Full disclosure: this journal has 31 devotionals (divided into 4 sections) that don't have to be completed in 30 consecutive days. If you take 60 days to finish, I won't tell.

Not only can you go at your own pace, but you can also complete the devotionals and journal prompts in any order you like. If you decide to color the pictures, you don't even have to color inside the lines.

This is your care-free, no judgement zone!

Date _____

Reflections

Are you and your husband on the same team? Why or Why not? What are three ways you can build or continue to build a team, even if you don't agree on everything?

_____
_____
_____
_____
_____
_____
_____
_____
_____
_____
_____
_____

Record the date so that you can look back and see where God brought you from

After reading the devotional and scripture, use the guided prompts to record your thoughts. Freely answer the questions as if no one else will ever read it.

Conversations with God

You do not have, because you do not ask
James 4: 2 - 3

Lord, I'm thankful for _____
_____
_____
_____
_____
_____

Lord, grant me _____
_____
_____
_____
_____
_____
_____

God's answer to my prayer: _____
_____
_____
_____

Date Received _____

Start each prayer with gratitude

Write your specific prayer needs as if God is reading every word

Record how God fulfilled your requests- and the date, so you'll always remember His faithfulness

How to Use this Book

Growing in love

Our challenges make us stronger!

LESSONS LEARNED

Write any lessons learned while going through the challenge so you'll know what to do next time

FAMILY INCIDENCES

Record any incidents, challenges, or trials your family may experience so that you can monitor growth, progress, and the miracles of God

SMALL VICTORIES

What were the small wins that you noticed during this time? Every little bit counts

And now your journey begins. If you go through this journal with a sincerity to hear God and to know His will for your family, I believe He will honor your efforts and meet you on these pages!

Table of Contents

Dear Stepmom,

You're not alone and you most certainly aren't crazy. What you're feeling is normal for anyone who's had their lives shaken by visitation schedules, EX's messes, and disagreements over discipline. I know what you're going through because I've walked 20 miles in your shoes. It wasn't easy, but with God's help, I survived and you can too!

This Journal was created to help you go from feeling:

hopeless, powerless, angry, frustrated, resentful, lost and wanting to give up

to feeling like

you're in control of your time, space, and most importantly, your emotions.

Welcome to your Retreat!

Here, you'll find a safe place to breathe, relax, and openly express yourself while sorting through your feelings.

No matter what you're facing, writing helps to combat feelings of overwhelm, so that you're better able to communicate and focus on solutions.

Don't worry.

Between you, God, and The Stepmom Retreat, I decree that your step-life will get better!

with Love,

Marcee

I. LORD, GRANT ME

"Lord, grant me the tools I need to stay on this journey. It gets hard and I want to give up. I wonder if I'm strong enough to handle the drama that comes with the responsibility. Sometimes I wonder if it's even worth it to stay."

Overwhelmed Stepmom

Wisdom

If any of you lacks wisdom, you should ask God

James 1: 5 niv

Thank God for the book sense or knowledge that we learn in school. It comes in handy when you need to figure out how much money to spend at the grocery store. But you can't use this knowledge to get kids to love and respect you. That requires wisdom.

Wisdom is the use of discernment to make consistently sound decisions. If you could get wisdom from textbooks, you wouldn't need God. You'd depend more on your books and less on Him. God doesn't want to be replaced by books. He longs to be your source of wisdom!

If you rely on your intelligence to fix situations, things can get messy, real quick. But if you go to Him, things can turn around, real quick.

Reflections

Have you ever taken matters into your own hands only to make them worse? If you could ask God for wisdom for any specific area, what would it be and why?

_____

_____

_____

_____

_____

_____

_____

_____

_____

_____

_____

_____

_____

_____

_____

_____

Conversations with God

You do not have, because you do not ask
James 4: 2 nkjv

Lord, I'm thankful for
_____
_____
_____
_____
_____
_____
_____

Lord, grant me
_____
_____
_____
_____
_____
_____
_____

God's answer to my prayer:
_____
_____
_____
_____

Date Received:
_____

Growing in love

Our challenges make us stronger!

LESSONS LEARNED

FAMILY INCIDENCES

SMALL VICTORIES

Forgiveness

If we confess our sins, he is faithful and just to forgive us our sins, and to cleanse us from all unrighteousness

1 John 1:9 nkjv

No matter what you've done, God is faithful to forgive you, if you simply confess.

He knows you're only human, yet He still loves you with an everlasting love. He longs for you to come to Him and pour out your guilty feelings.

There is no need to continue punishing yourself or holding yourself guilty. He says the moment you ask for forgiveness, He casts your sins into the sea of forgetfulness.

If the almighty God can forgive you, who are you to not forgive yourself?

Reflections

Is there anything that you can't seem to forgive yourself for?
Why not? Have you asked God to forgive you?

_____
_____
_____
_____
_____
_____
_____
_____
_____
_____
_____
_____
_____
_____
_____
_____
_____

Conversations with God

Whoever conceals their sins does not prosper,
but the one who confesses and renounces them finds mercy Proverbs 28:13 niv

Lord, I'm thankful for
_____
_____
_____
_____
_____
_____
_____

Lord, grant me
_____
_____
_____
_____
_____
_____

God's answer to my prayer:
_____
_____
_____
_____

Date Received:
_____

Growing in love

Our challenges make us stronger!

LESSONS LEARNED

FAMILY INCIDENCES

SMALL VICTORIES

Peace

The Lord will perfect that which concerns me

Psalm 138:8 nkjv

Worry is the exact opposite of peace. It's a skill that most women master because we are natural nurturers. Much in the same way we nurture the growth of babies, we nurture the growth of problems.

The more we think about our problems, the more we talk about them. The more we talk about them, the more they grow in our hearts. Before you know it, what was once a mole hill is now a full-grown mountain.

When the cares of this world come to rob you of peace, resist the urge to nurture them.

Exercise the privilege of being able to drop your problems at God's feet while you relax and join team #unBothered.

Date _____

Reflections

Close your eyes and imagine yourself lying on a beach, while giving God your concerns, one by one. What concerns are you giving Him? Why?

_____

_____

_____

_____

_____

_____

_____

_____

_____

_____

_____

_____

_____

_____

_____

_____

Conversations with God

Give all your worries and cares to God, for he cares about you
I Peter 5:7 nlt

Lord, I thank you for _____

_____

_____

_____

_____

_____

_____

Lord, grant me _____

_____

_____

_____

_____

_____

God's answer to my prayer: _____

_____

_____

_____

_____

Date Received: _____

Growing in love

Our challenges make us stronger!

LESSONS LEARNED

FAMILY INCIDENCES

SMALL VICTORIES

Patience

May the God of patience and comfort grant you to be like-minded toward one another...
Romans 15:5 nkjv

Because none of us will ever reach perfection, becoming Christ-like is an endless journey that every Christian takes. Some days are better than others. But the longer you stay on the journey, the closer you are to reaching your destination.

While on the journey, we are blessed to experience God's patience as He waits for us to grow in various areas of our lives. His patience is an example of the mercy that we are to show toward others.

Date _____

Reflections

Has God ever blessed you or shown you mercy at a time when you didn't feel like you deserved it? How can you extend the same mercy to others?

_____
_____
_____
_____
_____
_____
_____
_____
_____
_____
_____
_____
_____
_____
_____
_____

Conversations with God

The end of a matter is better than it's beginning, and patience is better than pride. Ecclesiastes 7:8 niv

Lord, I'm thankful for
_____
_____
_____
_____
_____
_____
_____

Lord, grant me
_____
_____
_____
_____
_____
_____
_____
_____

God's answer to my prayer:
_____
_____
_____
_____

Date received:
_____

Growing in love

Our challenges make us stronger!

LESSONS LEARNED

FAMILY INCIDENCES

SMALL VICTORIES

unConditional love

For God so loved the world that he gave his one and only Son, that whoever believes in him shall not perish but have eternal life

John 3:16 niv

God loves you and there's nothing you can do about it. You don't have to earn it or be perfect in order to experience His unconditional love that comes with no strings attached.

He did not wait for you to chose him or for you to get yourself together before He decided to love you.

Regardless of what you've done; who you did it to; or who you did it with, He loves you just because you're His child.

Date _____

Reflections

Have you ever done something that made you question whether or not God still loves you?
What does unconditional love mean to you?

_____

_____

_____

_____

_____

_____

_____

_____

_____

_____

_____

_____

_____

_____

_____

_____

Conversations with God

We love because he first loved us. 1 John 4:19 niv

Lord, I'm thankful for
_____
_____
_____
_____
_____
_____
_____

Lord, grant me
_____
_____
_____
_____
_____
_____
_____
_____
_____
_____

God's answer to my prayer:
_____
_____
_____
_____

Date received:
_____

Growing in love

Our challenges make us stronger!

LESSONS LEARNED

FAMILY INCIDENCES

SMALL VICTORIES

Joy

The joy of the Lord is your strength

Nehemiah 8:10 niv

You can grow weak in your faith if you allow an enemy to steal your joy.

One of the ways your joy is stolen is by stressing over people you can't control or change.

Being joyful is a choice. It doesn't just happen when everyone else around you becomes perfect. If that were the case, all of us would be depressed.

Joyfulness happens when you choose to smile and redirect your focus on the positive aspects of your life, in spite of your circumstances.

Date _____

Reflections

Do you spend a lot of time focusing on your problems? Why or why not? How does it make you feel? What should you focus on instead?

_____
_____
_____
_____
_____
_____
_____
_____
_____
_____
_____
_____
_____
_____
_____
_____
_____

Conversations with God

Ask and you will receive, so that your joy may be complete.
John 16:24 niv

Lord, I'm thankful for
_____
_____
_____
_____
_____
_____

Lord, grant me
_____
_____
_____
_____
_____
_____
_____
_____

God's answer to my prayer:
_____
_____
_____
_____

Date received:
_____

Growing in love

Our challenges make us stronger!

LESSONS LEARNED

FAMILY INCIDENCES

SMALL VICTORIES

Joy

emotional Healing

The Lord is near to the broken hearted

Psalm 34:18 nlt

Very few of us will escape life without having our hearts broken at some point. It's a painful reality that results from being in relationships with other flawed humans. Sometimes our parents, friends, or spouses are guilty. Harboring a broken heart it can hinder your relationships from growing.

But God specializes in fixing broken hearts!

That's the awesome reality that is the result of being in relationship with Him. He's the only one we can truly lean on who will never fail us.

He wants you to be honest and let Him put the pieces back together so that you can begin to heal and restore relationships.

Reflections

Are you struggling with the pain of a broken heart from a past or current relationship? Have you been honest about it with God? Why or Why not?

_____
_____
_____
_____
_____
_____
_____
_____
_____
_____
_____
_____
_____
_____
_____
_____
_____

Conversations with God

He heals the broken hearted and binds up their wounds

Psalm 147:3 niv

Lord, I'm thankful for
_____
_____
_____
_____
_____
_____
_____

Lord, grant me
_____
_____
_____
_____
_____
_____
_____
_____
_____

God's answer to my prayer:
_____
_____
_____
_____

Date received:
_____

Growing in love

Our challenges make us stronger!

LESSONS LEARNED

FAMILY INCIDENCES

SMALL VICTORIES

II. LORD, HELP ME

"Lord, help me. Sometimes I feel defeated. I don't want to feel this way, but the treatment I receive justifies my feelings. This life can be lonely. I feel invisible until somebody needs something from me.
I get tired of being the bigger person who has to overlook everyone else's problems for the sake of the kids. What about me?"

Frustrated Stepmom

Jealousy

A peaceful heart leads to a healthy body, but jealousy is like cancer in the bones

Proverbs 14:30 nlt

In a blended family, jealousy is likely to exist, especially if it appears that the kids are the top priority over everything and everyone else. These are natural feelings.

It's difficult for most adults to express negative emotions because many times we don't know how to express them without feeling judged. But expressing negative emotions, such as jealousy, can be lead to healing- if you do it in a positive way.

The more you're honest (with yourself) about your feelings, the better you're able to manage your feelings and ask for what you need in every relationship.

Reflections

Have you ever been jealous of anyone? Why? What would make you feel more secure in your relationships?

_____

_____

_____

_____

_____

_____

_____

_____

_____

_____

_____

_____

_____

_____

_____

Conversations with God

Heal me, Lord, and I will be healed

Jeremiah 17:14 niv

Lord, I'm thankful for
_____
_____
_____
_____
_____
_____

Lord, help me
_____
_____
_____
_____
_____
_____
_____
_____
_____

God's answer to my prayer:
_____
_____
_____
_____

Date received:
_____

Growing in love

Our challenges make us stronger!

LESSONS LEARNED

FAMILY INCIDENCES

SMALL VICTORIES

Anger

Don't sin by letting anger control you

Ephesians 4:26 nlt

Anger, in itself, is not a sin. It happens to all of us. Even Jesus expressed anger when he discovered the temple being used as "den of thieves," in Matthew 21.

Anger turns into sin when you lose control by saying or doing things that hurt others. At that point, you're being controlled by your emotions. If we didn't have the ability to control our emotions, God would never have told us to be angry without sinning.

Instead of loosing control, God wants us to use anger to inspire others to change, rather than provoking them to even the score.

Date _____

Reflections

Have you ever said or did something you regretted while you were angry? What could you have done instead?

_____

_____

_____

_____

_____

_____

_____

_____

_____

_____

_____

_____

_____

_____

_____

_____

_____

Conversations with God

The Lord is compassionate and gracious,
slow to anger, abounding in love Psalm 103:8 niv

Lord, I'm thankful for
_____
_____
_____
_____
_____
_____

Lord, help me
_____
_____
_____
_____
_____
_____
_____
_____

God's answer to my prayer:
_____
_____
_____
_____

Date Received:
_____

Growing in love

Our challenges make us stronger!

LESSONS LEARNED

FAMILY INCIDENCES

SMALL VICTORIES

Rejection

...If they persecuted me, they will persecute you also

John 15:20 niv

When car a manufacturer makes a vehicle, they put a lot of details into the design. They think of everything that will make the car functional for consumers. In the end, only the manufacturer can determine the car's value because they know exactly what it took to make the car special.

In the same way, God made you special. He put a lot of small details into your interior and exterior to make you a unique individual. As your creator, He's the only one who has the right to determine your value.

No one else's opinion matters.

P.S. He thinks you're pretty awesome.

Reflections

Have you ever felt unloved or unwanted? What was your response? Did it change the way you felt about yourself?

_____

_____

_____

_____

_____

_____

_____

_____

_____

_____

_____

_____

_____

_____

_____

_____

_____

Conversations with God

As you come to him, the living Stone—rejected by humans but chosen by God and precious to him 1 Peter 2:4 niv

Lord, I'm thankful for _____

_____

_____

_____

_____

_____

_____

Lord, help me _____

_____

_____

_____

_____

_____

_____

_____

_____

_____

God's answer to my prayer: _____

_____

_____

_____

_____

Date received: _____

Growing in love

Our challenges make us stronger!

LESSONS LEARNED

FAMILY INCIDENCES

SMALL VICTORIES

Anxiety

Do not be anxious about anything, but in every situation, by prayer and petition, with thanksgiving, present your requests to God

Philippians 4:6 niv

Anxiety is a form of excessive worry that is often triggered by unknown situations. The greatest source of anxiety comes from the need to control circumstances or outcomes so that the unknown becomes known.

The greatest solution for anxiety is learning to trust God with the outcome, no matter the situation. He promises that all things will work together for your good.

That's easier said than done because God doesn't always respond in the time or manner that we want Him to. It's at that point when we want to "help Him."

Instead of helping God, cooperate with Him by praying, trusting, and letting go.

Reflections

What causes you anxiety? What's the worst that can happen if you let go and allow God to take control?

_____

_____

_____

_____

_____

_____

_____

_____

_____

_____

_____

_____

_____

_____

_____

_____

Conversations with God

And we know that all things work together for good to them that love God
Romans 8:28 nlt

Lord, I'm thankful for

_____

_____

_____

_____

_____

_____

Lord, help me

_____

_____

_____

_____

_____

_____

_____

_____

_____

God's answer to my prayer:

_____

_____

_____

_____

Date received:

_____

Growing in love

Our challenges make us stronger!

LESSONS LEARNED

FAMILY INCIDENCES

SMALL VICTORIES

Fear

There is no fear in love but perfect love casts out all fear
1 John 4:18 niv

You can make your fears come to life by thinking about them over and over again. When the thought of possible outcomes becomes scarier than the actual outcome, you're allowing your thoughts to work against your faith.

But when you place blind trust in God's unfailing love for you, you're convinced that all things will work out for your good, even if the outcome is not what you expected.

God can use it to teach you something about Him and something about yourself.

P.S. There's nothing scarier than living without God

Reflections

Was there a time when you feared the outcome of something that never happened? How did it make you feel?

_____
_____
_____
_____
_____
_____
_____
_____
_____
_____
_____
_____
_____
_____
_____
_____
_____
_____

Conversations with God

For God has not given us a spirit of fear but of power and love and a sound mind 2 Timothy 1 :7 nkjv

Lord, I'm thankful for
_____
_____
_____
_____
_____
_____

Lord, help me
_____
_____
_____
_____
_____
_____
_____
_____

God's answer to my prayer:
_____
_____
_____
_____

Date received:
_____

Growing in love

Our challenges make us stronger!

LESSONS LEARNED

FAMILY INCIDENCES

SMALL VICTORIES

only
believe

Perfection

Not a single person on earth is always good and never sins

Ecclesiastes 7:20 nlt

Do you have a tendency to beat yourself up when you make mistakes?

There's nothing wrong with wanting to be excellent in your profession. But don't let perfection drive you to the point where you feel unworthy if you miss the mark in everything else. God loves you regardless.

The excessive need to be perfect actually drives you further away from His presence. It leads you to depend more on your ability to earn love or righteousness, than on Jesus' death.

Jesus died for flawed humans who need a savior. Jesus died just for you.

Reflections

Are you afraid to fail? Why or why not? How have you handled failure in your past?

_____

_____

_____

_____

_____

_____

_____

_____

_____

_____

_____

_____

_____

_____

_____

_____

Conversations with God

No one is good except God alone Mark 10:18 niv

Lord, I'm thankful for
_____
_____
_____
_____
_____
_____
_____

Lord, help me
_____
_____
_____
_____
_____
_____
_____
_____

God's answer to my prayer:
_____
_____
_____
_____

Date received:
_____

Growing in love

Our challenges make us stronger!

LESSONS LEARNED

FAMILY INCIDENCES

SMALL VICTORIES

taken for granted

Work willingly at whatever you do, as though you were working for the Lord rather than for people

Colossians 3:23 nlt

You may not always get the acknowledgement you deserve, but that doesn't mean that God doesn't see what you do and take notes.

When God sees your heart to serve and please Him, rest assured that He will not forget your faithfulness. His rewards are much greater than anything humans could ever do for you!

Keep doing the right thing, and watch Him work on your behalf.

Reflections

What makes you feel left out or taken for granted? What do you want to be acknowledge for and why?

_____
_____
_____
_____
_____
_____
_____
_____
_____
_____
_____
_____
_____
_____
_____
_____
_____

Conversations with God

your Father who sees in secret will Himself reward you
openly Matthew 6:4 nkjv

Lord, I'm thankful for
_____
_____
_____
_____
_____
_____

Lord, help me
_____
_____
_____
_____
_____
_____
_____
_____
_____

God's answer to my prayer:
_____
_____
_____
_____

Date received:
_____

Growing in love

Our challenges make us stronger!

LESSONS LEARNED

FAMILY INCIDENCES

SMALL VICTORIES

Resentment

Bless those who curse you, pray for those who mistreat you

Luke 6:28 niv

No one knows better than Jesus how hard it is to move forward when you've been lied on, lied to, or mistreated when you were only trying to do your best.

Yet, He still commands us to bless and pray for our enemies. Their actions are most likely a cry for help: a signal that something deeper is going on that has nothing to do with you. You're simply a convenient target.

You may never resolve the problem, if you stoop to their level. However, if you allow God to use you as a beacon of light, you'd be surprised at how He can turn the situation around to work in your favor.

Reflections

Who do you need to bless and pray for? Why?

_____

_____

_____

_____

_____

_____

_____

_____

_____

_____

_____

_____

_____

_____

_____

_____

_____

Conversations with God

Lord, I'm thankful for
_____
_____
_____
_____
_____
_____
_____

Lord, help me
_____
_____
_____
_____
_____
_____
_____
_____
_____

God's answer to my prayer:
_____
_____
_____
_____

Date received:
_____

Growing in love

Our challenges make us stronger!

LESSONS LEARNED

FAMILY INCIDENCES

SMALL VICTORIES

For additional support, visit
www.preparingtolove.com/stepmomchallenge/

Hopelessness

The righteous cry out, and the Lord hears them; he delivers them from all their troubles

Psalm 34:17 niv

There are times when our situations get so dark that we wonder if they're too big for God to handle. To make matters worse, God doesn't always come to our rescue when we want Him to. He only works in His timing. Not ours.

But He promises that if we keep our hope in Him, we won't be disappointed.

While you're waiting, focus on all the other times God has answered your prayers. If He did it before, He will do it again!

Reflections

What was the last thing you hoped for and how long did it take God to respond? What are you hoping for right now?

_____
_____
_____
_____
_____
_____
_____
_____
_____
_____
_____
_____
_____
_____
_____
_____
_____

Conversations with God

No one who hopes in you will ever be put to shame

Psalm 25:3 niv

Lord, I'm thankful for
_____
_____
_____
_____
_____
_____

Lord, help me
_____
_____
_____
_____
_____
_____
_____
_____

God's answer to my prayer:
_____
_____
_____
_____

Date received:
_____

Growing in love

Our challenges make us stronger!

LESSONS LEARNED

FAMILY INCIDENCES

SMALL VICTORIES

III. LORD, TEACH ME

"Lord, teach me to know you and to honor your commandments. I want you to be pleased with me but I'm not ever sure if I'm doing the right thing. I work hard to make everyone happy, still it's not enough."

Desperate Stepmom

Faith

Without faith it's impossible to please God
Hebrews 11:6 niv

The roads we travel can sometimes be so dark that we can't see where we're going. That's when we have to let go of our "normal" route and trust God to lead.

If you've ever had to trust God to get you somewhere, you know that means you have to follow the all the detours and pit stops that He wants you to take. That's never fun, especially if you have preconceived ideas of where you should go and how fast you should get there.

But, if you walk by faith and let Him do what only He can do, you'll know what it's like to really be a child of God; as opposed to just another Christian who will go to heaven, one day, but will never experience heaven on earth.

Date_____

Reflections

What are you having difficulty believing God for? Why is it hard to trust God?

_____
_____
_____
_____
_____
_____
_____
_____
_____
_____
_____
_____
_____
_____
_____
_____

Conversations with God

With God, all things are possible
Matthew 19:26 niv

Lord, I'm thankful for
_____
_____
_____
_____
_____
_____

Lord, teach me
_____
_____
_____
_____
_____
_____
_____
_____

God's answer to my prayer:
_____
_____
_____
_____

Date received:

Growing in love

Our challenges make us stronger!

LESSONS LEARNED

FAMILY INCIDENCES

SMALL VICTORIES

the Father

your father knows exactly what you need before you ask Him

Matthew 6:8 niv

If your earthly father was negligent or missing in action, that can make it harder for you to see God as your daddy. But a distorted view doesn't change who He is and who He wants to be in your life.

He wants to be more than a savior. When you're hurt, confused, lonely, and feeling hopeless, climb into his arms as ask Him to comfort you. When you have a need or when you're afraid, tell Him all about it.

No problem is too big or too small. He longs to be there for you in every way, but His hands are tied as long as you limit Him to only being your savior.

Reflections

As a child what was your relationship like with your biological father? How did that affect your ability to trust God to be father?

_____

_____

_____

_____

_____

_____

_____

_____

_____

_____

_____

_____

_____

_____

_____

_____

_____

Conversations with God

...how much more will your Father in heaven give good things to those who ask Him Matthew 7:11 niv

Lord, I'm thankful for

_____

_____

_____

_____

_____

_____

Lord, teach me

_____

_____

_____

_____

_____

_____

_____

_____

God's answer to my prayer:

_____

_____

_____

_____

Date received:

_____

Growing in love

Our challenges make us stronger!

LESSONS LEARNED

FAMILY INCIDENCES

SMALL VICTORIES

to Forgive

If you refuse to forgive others, your father will not forgive you

Matthew 6:15 nlt

Forgiveness is a gift that you give yourself. The more you let go of offenses, the more freedom you experience; the more forgiveness you receive when you need it; and the more Christ-like you become.

True forgiveness means the offender no longer owes retribution or apologies for the offenses they've committed. Though it would be nice if they showed remorse, God's love, forgives regardless.

It's easier said than done, especially when someone continually goes out of their way to hurt you. But the person who commits the most offenses, is often the person who needs the most love.

Reflections

Have you ever hurt someone else-intentionally or unintentionally- and wished that you hadn't done it? Is there anyone you need to forgive right now? Why?

_____
_____
_____
_____
_____
_____
_____
_____
_____
_____
_____
_____
_____
_____
_____
_____

Conversations with God

Be kind and compassionate to one another, forgiving each other, just as in Christ, God forgave you Ephesians 4:32 niv

Lord, I'm thankful for
_____
_____
_____
_____
_____
_____
_____

Lord, teach me
_____
_____
_____
_____
_____
_____
_____

God's answer to my prayer:
_____
_____
_____
_____

Date Received:

Growing in love

Our challenges make us stronger!

LESSONS LEARNED

FAMILY INCIDENCES

SMALL VICTORIES

to Love

The greatest of these is love

1Corinthians 13:13 niv

Love is demonstrated by what you do, more so than what you say.

It's not just a feeling that you get when you see someone special. Because feelings can change based on our mood, the weather, or any other unstable factor. We have to make a decision to love that's based on our daily walk with Christ.

Love is a kind, merciful act that's directed towards people, even if they don't deserve it.
After all, that's what God does for us.

Reflections

Is there someone you need to show more love to? How can you show love to them in a way they would appreciate?

_____

_____

_____

_____

_____

_____

_____

_____

_____

_____

_____

_____

_____

_____

_____

_____

Conversations with God

Beloved, if God so loved us, we ought also to love one another
1 John 4:11 nkjv

Lord, I'm thankful for
_____
_____
_____
_____
_____
_____
_____

Lord, teach me
_____
_____
_____
_____
_____
_____
_____
_____

God's answer to my prayer:
_____
_____
_____
_____

Date Received:
_____

Growing in love

Our challenges make us stronger!

LESSONS LEARNED

FAMILY INCIDENCES

SMALL VICTORIES

Grace

My grace is sufficient for you
II Corinthians 12:9 nkjv

A healthy dose of grace can empower you to do any and all things through Christ—even if you're inexperienced or lack the qualifications. Grace is a gift that you don't deserve, but it's one that you can receive if you ask.

Instead of saying, "I can't take it anymore," when life hits hard, ask God for His grace so that you can do those things supernaturally.

You can ask for God's grace to succeed; to be a stepmom; to be a wife; to conduct business; to do whatever it is you have to get done today.

Reflections

Have you ever surprised yourself by doing something you never though was possible? What do you need God's grace for today?

_____
_____
_____
_____
_____
_____
_____
_____
_____
_____
_____
_____
_____
_____
_____

Conversations with God

Let us approach God's throne of grace with confidence, so that we may receive mercy and find grace to help us in our time of need

Hebrews 4:16 niv

Lord, I'm thankful for _____

_____

_____

_____

_____

_____

_____

Lord, teach me _____

_____

_____

_____

_____

_____

_____

_____

God's answer to my prayer: _____

_____

_____

_____

Date Received: _____

Growing in love

Our challenges make us stronger!

LESSONS LEARNED

FAMILY INCIDENCES

SMALL VICTORIES

Faithfulness

Let us hold fast the confession of our hope without wavering, for He who promised is faithful

Hebrews 10:23 nkjv

A faithful person is one who keeps her promises, over and over again. She does what he says she will do every time. You never have to question whether or not she means what she says. You can fully trust a faithful person.

As humans, no matter how hard we try to keep every promise, there will be times when we fail; we're not perfect.

But God is faithful. You may never know how he does it or when He'll do it, but if you ask according to his will, you can be assured that hears you and he'll do what he promised.

Reflections

Have you ever broken a promise? What promise do you need God to fulfill right now?

_____

_____

_____

_____

_____

_____

_____

_____

_____

_____

_____

_____

_____

_____

_____

_____

_____

Conversations with God

If we ask anything according to His will, He hears us
1 John 5:14 nkjv

Lord, I'm thankful for
_____
_____
_____
_____
_____
_____
_____

Lord, teach me
_____
_____
_____
_____
_____
_____
_____
_____

God's answer to my prayer:
_____
_____
_____
_____

Date Received:
_____

Growing in love

Our challenges make us stronger!

LESSONS LEARNED

FAMILY INCIDENCES

SMALL VICTORIES

IV. LORD, HELP US

For additional support, visit
www.preparingtolove.com/stepmomchallenge/

"Lord, help us to fight together and not fight each other. Sometimes it feels like my husband is my biggest enemy. He doesn't understand why I feel like an outsider in this family. In fact, no one understands. I have no one to talk to and I'm starting to wonder why I'm still here."

Lonely Stepmom

Teammates

Two are better than one for they can help each other succeed

Ecclesiastes 4:9 nlt

Have you ever felt like it was "you against them?" In blended families, it's natural for biological parents to take sides with their children. But the strongest partnership should always be between husband and wife. If they're not on the same team, the opposition wins, every time.

Teammates have clearly defined roles. They support, encourage, and comfort each other-- even if one of them fumbles.

The most powerful example of this is found in 1 Samuel 18 - 20. The bond between David and Jonathan was so strong that not even Jonathan's father, King Saul, was able to destroy it.

If parents form a comparable team, they present a fortress so strong that no devil in hell can destroy it!

Reflections

Are you and your husband on the same team? Why or Why not? What are three ways you can build or continue to build a team, even if you don't agree on everything?

_____
_____
_____
_____
_____
_____
_____
_____
_____
_____
_____
_____
_____
_____
_____
_____

Conversations with God

There is no 'I in team, but there is in WIN
~Michael Jordan

Lord, I'm thankful for
_____
_____
_____
_____
_____
_____
_____

Lord, help us
_____
_____
_____
_____
_____
_____
_____

God's answer to my prayer:
_____
_____
_____
_____

Date Received:
_____

Growing in love

Our challenges make us stronger!

LESSONS LEARNED

FAMILY INCIDENCES

SMALL VICTORIES

Disicipline

For the Lord corrects those he loves, just as a father corrects a child in whom he delights
Proverbs 3:12 nlt

Kids crave discipline —whether they know it or not. That's the best indication they have of how much their parents love them. Without discipline, they may as well be left alone to raise themselves.

God, our father, would never leave us alone and without guidance. That would make Him a negligent parent. As a good father, He's more concerned with our character development than our earthly desires.

To ensure that we develop character, He has clearly defined commandments, laws, and consequences to help us understand what's expected of us.

The more your kids understand the expectations, the easier it is to enforce consequences.

Reflections

What are the rules and consequences that should be established in your home? Have you communicated them with your husband? Your kids?

_____

_____

_____

_____

_____

_____

_____

_____

_____

_____

_____

_____

_____

_____

_____

_____

Conversations with God

...A child left to himself brings his mother to shame
Proverbs 29:15 kjv

Lord, I thank you for _____

_____

_____

_____

_____

_____

_____

Lord, help us _____

_____

_____

_____

_____

_____

_____

_____

God's answer to my prayer: _____

_____

_____

_____

_____

Date Received: _____

Growing in love

Our challenges make us stronger!

LESSONS LEARNED

FAMILY INCIDENCES

SMALL VICTORIES

Boundaries

Do not let your foot be in your neighbor's house too much, or he may become tired of you

Proverbs 25:17 nlv

Boundaries are the limits that you place around your relationships, your family, and your physical space that tell others how far they can go and how often. Without boundaries, your home could easily be dictated by those who don't live there or pay bills there.

In a blended family, sometimes you have to place limits on in-laws, former in-laws, EX's, and even the children.

Boundaries can be as simple as turning your phone off after hours; or complex by not allowing disrespectful people in your home.

If your family structure is consistently being threatened, you owe it to yourself to protect it by setting clear boundaries.

Reflections

What are some boundaries that you can establish to protect your family? Your space? Your time?

_____

_____

_____

_____

_____

_____

_____

_____

_____

_____

_____

_____

_____

_____

_____

_____

Growing in love

Our challenges make us stronger!

LESSONS LEARNED

FAMILY INCIDENCES

SMALL VICTORIES

Conversations with God

Setting boundaries is about having the courage to love ourselves even when we risk disappointing others ~Brene Brown

Lord, I'm thankful for

_____

_____

_____

_____

_____

_____

_____

Lord, help us

_____

_____

_____

_____

_____

_____

_____

God's answer to my prayer:

_____

_____

_____

_____

Date Received:

For additional support, visit
www.preparingtolove.com/stepmomchallenge/

Money

God is able to do much more than we ask or think (about asking) through His power working in us
Ephesians 3:20 nlv

Child support, shared financial responsibilities with EX's, and different spending philosophies can all cause blended families to come up short.

One of the reasons we fight about money is because we fear running out or not having enough to go around.

The energy that we spend fighting our spouse is better spent praying to an all-knowing, all-sufficient God who hears our every cry. No problem is too big or small for you to talk to Him about.

He's waiting on you to trust Him with your entire life- not just the things you think you can't handle, but everything.

Date _____

Reflections

Have you prayed about any financial worries? Why or why not?
What's stopping you from trusting God with your finances?

_____
_____
_____
_____
_____
_____
_____
_____
_____
_____
_____
_____
_____
_____
_____
_____
_____

Conversations with God

your Father knows exactly what you need even before you ask him
Matthew 6:8 nlt

Lord, I'm thankful for
_____
_____
_____
_____
_____
_____
_____

Lord, help us
_____
_____
_____
_____
_____
_____
_____
_____

God's answer to my prayer:
_____
_____
_____
_____

Date received:
_____

Growing in love

Our challenges make us stronger!

LESSONS LEARNED

FAMILY INCIDENCES

SMALL VICTORIES

Conflict

What causes fights and quarrels among you? Don't they come from your desires that battle within you?

James 4:1 niv

More often than not, when you're in consistent conflict with someone else, God is trying to teach you something about yourself.

Interactions that cause you to become angry, defensive, or withdrawn are often the result of buried wounds that may or may not have anything to do with the person you're in conflict with.

The most effective path to healing is to go before God and honestly judge yourself and your motives. Open your wounds and allow Him to pour a spiritual balm on them.

Date _____

Reflections

Are you involved in consistent conflict with your husband or anyone else? What can you learn about yourself through this conflict?

_____
_____
_____
_____
_____
_____
_____
_____
_____
_____
_____
_____
_____
_____
_____
_____
_____

Conversations with God

If it is possible, as far as it depends on you, live at peace with everyone
Romans 12:18 niv

Lord, I'm thankful for

_____

_____

_____

_____

_____

_____

_____

Lord, help us

_____

_____

_____

_____

_____

_____

_____

God's answer to my prayer:

_____

_____

_____

_____

Date Received:

Growing in love

Our challenges make us stronger!

LESSONS LEARNED

FAMILY INCIDENCES

SMALL VICTORIES

Agreement

If two of you on earth agree about anything they ask for, it will be done for them

Matthew 18:19 niv

Gaining agreement is the best thing you can do with your husband, but most of the time, it won't happen automatically. When you bring two people, with valid, but different, perspectives together, there has to be a middle ground.

The middle ground is found through negotiation and compromise in those areas that you disagree.

The more you can gain agreement, the more your prayers will get answered and the more your marriage wins!

Reflections

What areas do you disagree with your husband? What are some ways you can compromise so that your marriage wins?

_____

_____

_____

_____

_____

_____

_____

_____

_____

_____

_____

_____

_____

_____

_____

_____

_____

_____

Conversations with God

Can two people walk together without agreeing on the direction?
Amos 3:3 nlt

Lord, I'm thankful for
_____
_____
_____
_____
_____
_____
_____

Lord, help us
_____
_____
_____
_____
_____
_____
_____
_____

God's answer to my prayer:
_____
_____
_____
_____

Date Received:
_____

Growing in love

Our challenges make us stronger!

LESSONS LEARNED

FAMILY INCIDENCES

SMALL VICTORIES

Communication

Tune your ears to wisdom,
and concentrate on
understanding
Proverbs 2:2 nlt

Communication is easier when you're on neutral grounds. But in the middle of a disagreement, it's nearly impossible to talk and hear each other. Most of the times we're listening just to give a reply--not necessarily to understand.

When we intentionally listen to gain understanding, we can develop empathy and see things from the other person's perspective. We can better comprehend why our partner feels a certain way and be more open to the solution.

Reflections

What was the last misunderstanding that you had with your husband? Did you attempt to understand his position? Why or Why not?

_____
_____
_____
_____
_____
_____
_____
_____
_____
_____
_____
_____
_____
_____
_____
_____
_____

Conversations with God

The greatest distance between two people is a misunderstanding ~Unknown

Lord, I'm thankful for _____

_____

_____

_____

_____

_____

Lord, help us _____

_____

_____

_____

_____

_____

_____

_____

God's answer to my prayer: _____

_____

_____

_____

_____

Date received: _____

Growing in love

Our challenges make us stronger!

LESSONS LEARNED

FAMILY INCIDENCES

SMALL VICTORIES

custody Battles

"Be still, and know that I am God

Psalm 46:10 niv

Many times, custody battles have more to do with maintaining control or exerting power over other adults, than they do the welfare of the children.

Real power comes from letting go and asking God to take over. If you step out of the fight, your opponent will have no one to fight but themselves.

Initially, it will be hard to watch kids go back and forth to a home you may feel is unstable and insecure; it will be hard to maintain the stance of a mature adult when children are being turned against you.

But, when you let go and pray for God's best in this situation, you're opening yourself up for a miracle.

You have all the power you need in your prayer closet.

Reflections

What is God asking you to let go of today? What would it look like for you to "be still" and let God handle the situation?

_____

_____

_____

_____

_____

_____

_____

_____

_____

_____

_____

_____

_____

_____

_____

_____

_____

Conversations with God

The Lord himself will fight for you; Just stay calm
Exodus 14:14 nlt

Lord, I'm thankful for
_____
_____
_____
_____
_____
_____

Lord, help us
_____
_____
_____
_____
_____
_____
_____
_____
_____

God's answer to my prayer:
_____
_____
_____
_____
_____

Date received:
_____

Growing in love

Our challenges make us stronger!

LESSONS LEARNED

FAMILY INCIDENCES

SMALL VICTORIES

the Praying Wife

The heart of the king is like rivers of water in the hand of the Lord. He turns it where He wishes

Proverbs 21:1 nlv

Wouldn't it be great if your husband did everything right all the time? If he did, he wouldn't be a husband, he'd be a robot. And, you just can't get the same level of love and affection from a robot as you can a husband.

Instead of arguing with him or correcting him, let go and allow God to work in his life. Completely release yourself from torment of stress that comes from trying to fix him.

Spend your time in prayer and watch God turn his heart as easily as He turns water!

Date _____

Reflections

If you could change anything about your husband, what would it be? Have you prayed about it? Why or why not?

_____
_____
_____
_____
_____
_____
_____
_____
_____
_____
_____
_____
_____
_____
_____
_____
_____
_____

Conversations with God

She brings him good, not harm, all the days of her life

Proverbs 31: 12 niv

Lord, I'm thankful for
_____
_____
_____
_____
_____
_____

Lord, help us
_____
_____
_____
_____
_____
_____
_____
_____

God's answer to my prayer:
_____
_____
_____
_____

Date received:
_____

Growing in love

Our challenges make us stronger!

LESSONS LEARNED

FAMILY INCIDENCES

SMALL VICTORIES

For additional support, visit
www.preparingtolove.com/stepmomchallenge/

Marcee Woodard

About the author

Marcee Woodard is a Christian Counselor, wife, mom, and bonus mom who lives in West Tennessee with her husband, four kids, and a needy golden doodle. For more information, visit her blog, preparingtolove.com.

.

www.ingramcontent.com/pod-product-compliance
Lightning Source LLC
LaVergne TN
LVHW051739080426
835511LV00018B/3149